LOST IN INFORMATION

This little book is the concept and creation of Norwegian artist Astrid Iverslien. As an art teacher, she has worked with children in secondary schools for several decades and has seen the rapid impact of social media in society and the changes it has produced, both good and bad. Astrid has previously illustrated several books for children; her latest 'Astrid & the War' depicts her childhood spent in Norway during Nazi occupation. She has practised daily meditation for 45 years and deeply believes in its healing powers and a path back to oneself.

LOST IN INFORMATION

E R
PUBLISHING

The Stories,
41 Panmure Road,
London
SE26 6NB, U.K.

Published by ER Publishing Ltd, 2023

Copyright ©Astrid Iverslien

All rights reserved
Without limiting the rights under copyright reserved above, no part of this publication may be reproduced, stored in or introduced into a retrieval system, or transmitted in any form or by any means, electronic, mechanical, photocopying, recording, or otherwise, without the written permission of the publisher, except in the case of brief quotations embodied in critical articles and reviews.

Illustrations © Astrid Iverslien

Printed in the U.K by Imprintdigital.com Seychelles Farm, Upton Pyne, EX5 5HY, UK
A CIP catalogue record for this book is available at the British Library
ISBN: 978-1-3999-6614-6

The moral right of the author has been asserted. All characters and events in this publication, other than those clearly in the public domain, are fictitious and any resemblance to real persons, living or dead, is purely coincidental.

www.erpublishme.com

FOR
SASKIA & HARPER

*'Where is the wisdom
we have lost in knowledge?
Where is the knowledge
we have lost in information?'*

T.S. ELIOT

DIGITAL POWER: The large technological firms are forming tomorrow's world order.

The opportunity of technology to unite or split people, has gone a long way since the first telephone conversation between America and Europe came in 1940. Some might say, too far in our 24/7/365 connectedness.

When the internet arrived, we were promised a world of unstoppable information, an endless library: it was a gateway to freedom.

The sad part is that a child in front of a smartphone feels more like burning down a library. Their eyes have lost their sparkle; they become passive, dragged into a world they cannot influence or create. This is not progress but a race toward the abyss.

Mixed reality blindfolds you,
closing the real world out.

You enter an alternative digital world:
a passive existence, a caged tragedy.

I am dead scared of my obsession, hooked as I am on scrolling, on and on it goes, scrolling, scrolling... I am scared I am losing my concentration. Scared of my wasted hours, scared of my sad life of watching millions of images and 15 second videos.

But how can I stop it? How can I return to real life? To tangible objects, to a person's gaze?

HELP!
I want my old life back!

I used to go on beautiful outings, now I am drowning in my smartphone. I am out of control, making superficial friendships and scrolling endlesly. At the end of the day, I am anxious, depressed and sad.

I hear ADHD is more prevalent. We have our hearts and minds in our phones and barely have our feet in reality.

I have been robbed of my concentration. Once upon a time, I used to read a lot of books. Now I don't have time. Instead, I spend an average of seven hours a day on my phone.

Rediscover the enchantment of
reading books.

The brilliance of it,
the solitude of it,
the power, the joy.

DISTRACTED PARENTING:
A mother disappearing into her phone as her child waits desperately for her attention.

Your smartphone habits are affecting your children. Humans develop best through interaction. Researchers conclude that the gaze is a powerful signal to a child. It says that the parenting is available and that you are interested in communicating, and the child in return, will make a greater attempt at interacting.

LOOK AT ME!

A generation of bent necked children might grow up to one day see their osteopath in a similar light to their phone: as someone with all the answers.

MULTI-TASKING:
E-scooters, mobile devices and headphones.

Where is the concentration to protect yourself from the danger of the road?

All of our senses are there to help us navigate life safely, they are not to be ignored.

Lost in information
that entangles us like
a spider's web.

Sometimes we simply have to close our eyes in order to see better.

MEDITATION is not just an age-old practice reserved for monks or spiritual gurus; it's a sanctuary for the modern soul. By disconnecting, even if just for a few minutes daily, and sinking into meditation, you grant yourself the profound gift of presence. You cultivate a space where your mind can breathe, free from the chokehold of algorithms and updates. Meditation bolsters concentration, sharpens intuition, and ignites a deeper connection to the world around you—reminding you that life's most captivating moments are not happening in the palm of your hand, but right before your very eyes. So, unplug and dive inward. In the silent echoes of meditation, you might just find the most authentic version of yourself.

When we have the opportunity, a meditation in nature opens our senses in a quiet way to discover and be present in the enormity that surrounds us.

If you are sitting long enough by the riverside, you will see clearer than ever before.

A JOURNEY BACK TO YOURSELF

MINDFULNESS MEDITATION: This is simply about being present. Sit comfortably, close your eyes, and focus on your breathing.
When your mind wanders—and it will— gently bring it back to your breath. It's about observing your thoughts without judgment.

BODY SCAN MEDITATION: Lie down and focus on different parts of your body, one at a time. Start with your toes and move up to your head. Notice any sensations, tension, or warmth in each area.

LOVING-KINDNESS MEDITATION: This is about cultivating compassion. Sit comfortably, close your eyes, and envision sending love and well-wishes to yourself, then to loved ones, and gradually to the entire world. It's a heart-filling practice.

WALKING MEDITATION: Find a quiet place to walk, like a park or garden. Focus on each step, feeling the ground beneath your feet and the rhythm of your movements. It combines physical activity with mindfulness.

BREATH AWARENESS OR ZEN MEDITATION: Simply focus on your breath. Breathe in and out naturally, noticing the rise and fall of your chest and belly. If your mind drifts, return to concentrating on your breathing.

MANTRA MEDITATION: Choose a word or phrase that is meaningful to you (like "peace" or "I am calm"). Sit comfortably and repeat your mantra either out loud or in your mind.

ACEM MEDITATION: A journey back to yourself. Acem meditation is a simple meditation technique for relaxation, increased energy, improved health and personal growth.

Remember, there is no "right way to meditate. The key is to find a method that feels right for you and to practice regularly, even if it's just for a few minutes each day. Over time, you will likely notice increased clarity, calmness, and focus in your daily life. Your phone will no longer be such a temptation.